Israel and Middle East

Past Present Future
הגיע הזמן לנצח

■ ■ ■

By Prince Handley

University of Excellence Press

Copyright © 2016 by Prince Handley
All Rights Reserved.

UNIVERSITY OF EXCELLENCE PRESS
San Diego ◾ London ◾ Tel Aviv

ISBN-13: 978-0692612637
ISBN-10: 0692612637

Second Edition

The only Israel · Middle East book you need!

TABLE OF CONTENTS

FOREWORD

How would you like to walk through the **real sequence** of events concerning the original Children of Israel—and to discover their real history.

You will in this book ... AND ... you will learn the factual and undisputed boundaries—**specific description of the land**—given to the People of Israel.

You will discover the G-d designed significance of the meaning "Hebrew" and its connection to Abraham AND the Promised Land.

In addition, you will learn the significance of **current—*and future*—geopolitical happenings that play upon Israel—and the Middle East—**now and in the future.

What prophetic significance does Turkey, Islam, ISIS, the New World Governance and Iraq have in relation to Israel? You will find out in this book.

But, more importantly, you will learn what to watch for—*and to expect*—from the United Nations ... AND from the New World Governance.

You will learn G-d's plan for Israel: NOW and in the future. **You will learn future news NOW!**

Israel and Middle East

Past Present Future
הגיע הזמן לנצח

■ ■ ■

ORIGIN OF THE JEWISH PEOPLE
AND THE LAND OF ISRAEL

In the Brit Chadashah—the New Testament—in Acts 17:26, the Bible says, "(G-d) has made of one blood all nations of men for to dwell on all the face of the earth, and has **determined the times** before appointed, **and the boundaries** of their habitations."

From one man—Adam—G-d has made every nation of men to scatter and settle on the whole face of the earth. G-d knowing beforehand which nations would rise and fall and at what time they would be in power. G-d also fixed their boundaries ahead of time for these certain periods of time.

The first of eleven colleges and universities I attended I received my B.S.I.E. and later worked for 18 months in civil engineering work with my own surveying crew. We dealt meticulously with **boundaries and land descriptions**.

G-d **established the boundaries of the nation of Israel** about 4000 years ago, during the time of Abraham.

On the same day **the LORD made a covenant with Abram**, saying:

> *"To your descendants I have given this land, from the river of Egypt to the great river, the River Euphrates—* the land of the Kenites, the Kenezzites, the Kadmonites, the Hittites, the

Perizzites, the Rephaim, the Amorites, the Canaanites, the Girgashites, and the Jebusites."

Torah: *Bereshith* / Genesis 15:18-21

The description of borders was an important part of the ancient royal land grants. So you can see that the East to West boundaries of the land promised to Abraham's descendants extends from the Euphrates River to the river—or, brook—of Egypt.***

***It is debated whether the "river" of Egypt, the Wadi el Arish in northeastern Sinai (Numbers 34:5), or the eastern branch of the Nile delta is in view. See 1 Kings 4:21.

About 500 years later—*around 1,500 B.C.E.*—G-d gave the **description of the boundaries of Israel in more detail** in relation to tribal areas to Moshe (Moses)—but only as far as Moses could see with his eyes.

"And Moses went up from the plains of Moab unto the mountain of Nebo, to the top of Pisgah that is over against Jericho. And the LORD showed him all the land of Gilead unto Dan,

And all Naphtali, and the land of Ephraim, and Manasseh, and all the land of Judah, unto the utmost sea,

And the south, and the plain of the valley of Jericho, the city of palm trees, unto Zoar.

And the LORD *said unto him,* **This is the land which I swore unto Abraham, unto Isaac, and unto Jacob, saying, I will give it unto your descendants***: I have caused you to see it with your eyes, but you shalt not go over there."*

Torah: *Devarim* / Deuteronomy 34:1-12

Abraham had two sons: Ishmael and Isaac. (Read Torah: Genesis Chapters 16, 17, 21, and 22.) Ishmael was Abraham's son by his Egyptian maid, Hagar. Ishmael became the "father" of the Arab nations; he was the son "of the flesh", not the son which G-d had promised to Abraham. **Isaac was the "son of the promise"**, but Ishmael was the result of Abraham trying to "help G-d out"—trying to help G-d keep His word. **Have you ever tried to do this? Have you ever acted too quickly instead of waiting with patience for the promise of G-d to come to pass?**

In Genesis 21:12, G-d said unto Abraham, *"in Isaac shall your seed be called."* **Through the line of Isaac the promised "seed" would come who would bless the world.** Isaac had twin sons named Esau and Jacob. Even though Jacob was the younger, he inherited the blessing—or "birthright"—from his father Isaac (Torah: *Bereshith* / Genesis 25:19-34).

Jacob's name was changed to Israel on an occasion after he had wrestled with an angel of G-d all night (Torah: Genesis Chapter 32). **The name "Jacob" means "heel catcher" or "supplanter"—one who displaces, as Jacob did to his brother Esau in regard to the birthright. The name Israel means "having power with G-d" or "G-d's fighter."** A change had happened in Jacob's life; he began to see the purpose of G-d for his life! **Have you had a change in your life?** Do you have a vision of what G-d wants you to do? If so, you will be changed! This change doesn't have to take place when you're young. It might be after you've "weathered" the years—or rather, after the years have "weathered" you!

9

The G-d of Israel is the G-d of Abraham, Isaac, and Jacob. Jacob—whose name was changed to Israel—had 12 sons who became the heads of the 12 tribes of Israel. Now you see where the nation of Israel came from: from the seed of Abraham, starting with Abraham's grandson, Jacob. **Jacob (Israel) was the father of the 12 tribes**. G-d called Abraham out and he became a blessing to the whole earth through his obedience. **It was through his (Abraham's) seedline that Yeshua came. Abraham produced a nation—*Israel*—and that nation produced the Messiah: Yeshua HaMashiach (Jesus, the Anointed One).**

The name "Jew" was first used to refer to someone from the tribe of Judah. Later, **after** the return from the 70 year captivity in Babylon—*in the time of Ezra and Nehemiah*—the name "Jew" was used to refer to anyone from any of the 12 tribes. However, the tribe of Judah seemed to make up the larger portion of the remnant of Israel. The children of Israel were originally called "Hebrews." In the Brit Chadasha—*the New Testament*—Rabbi Shaul (the apostle Paul) was called a Hebrew; and yet the two terms, "Hebrew" and "Jew", are now used with little distinction.

Concerning the term "Hebrew," it is interesting that after the Children of Israel finished wandering for 40 years, and **before they passed over the Jordan River into the Promised Land**, they lodged for three days at the brink of the Jordan River. Joshua, their leader after Moshe, sent officers through the camp who commanded the people as follows:

*"When you see the ark of the covenant of the LORD your G-d, and the priests—the Levites—bearing it, then you shall set out from your place and go after it. Yet there shall be a space between you and the ark, about 2,000 cubits (1,000 yards or 914 meters) by measure. Do not come near the ark, so that you may know the way by which you must go, for you have not **passed** this way before."* (Tanakh: Sefer Y'hoshua / Joshua 3:1-4)

The Hebrew root word for "**passed**" used above is "**abar**" [ah-var] which means "**to pass over, go through, pass beyond, or to make a transition** [figuratively or literally]."

To arrive INSIDE your Promised Land, you will have to go through a TRANSITION! The Hebrew word "abar" also means **"to pass from one side to the other side."**

Interestingly enough, **a derivative of the word "abar" is "ibriy" which means "Hebrew"** and is the **ethnic description of Abraham and his seed line**, who was **a descendant of "Eber"**—the great grandson of Noah's son Shem.

Genesis 14:13 / *Bereshith* talks about **"Abram the Hebrew."** Exodus 7:16 / *Shemot* mentions **"the LORD God of the Hebrews."** Here "Hebrews" represents a tribe of Semites (sons of Shem).

Abraham "crossed over" the Euphrates River from Haran to Canaan, the land God promised him. **How did he do it—through OBEDIENCE!** Abraham, his wife Sarah, and his nephew Lot had originally left Ur of the Chaldees with his father, Terah, and arrived in Haran. It's possible the LORD had wanted Terah to take the trip of faith from Haran and he may not have obeyed; possibly that is why G-d chose Abraham.

PROPHETICAL IMPORTANCE OF THE WAR IN IRAQ FOR ISRAEL AND MIDDLE EAST

The *extended* war in Iraq played—*and will continue to play*—an important part in End Time prophecy: **for Israel, for the Middle East ...** *and for the West*. The result will be a **paradigm shift in world commerce, politics and religion**. Plus ... **Israel will be swept up in a vortex of persecution.**

Right now, Iraq plays a key piece—not only in the Middle East with the "tug of war" between ISIS and Iran—but in the prophetic puzzle (and the timeline) of the world.

Men wage war, but G-d wages eternal justice. The real reason behind the war in Iraq—unknown to men—is for clearing the way to rebuild Babylon: NEW BABYLON.

Babylon, in the land of Shinar, was the headquarters of the first world autocrat. His name was "Nimrod." Scripture—*in the original Hebrew language, and also supported by rabbis*—shows that **Nimrod was "a mighty hunter against—***or in opposition to***—the LORD."** (See Torah, *Bereshith* / Genesis 10:8-9)

Just as Babylon was the headquarters for the first world dictator, so the NEW BABYLON will be the headquarters of the FINAL world dictator, a despot and worse than tyrant. He will be chosen by the New World Order (or whatever name the organization ascribes to itself at that time). He will be the FALSE messiah and the greatest enemy that Israel and the Jewish People have ever known.

Babylon, in Iraq, lies 85 km or 55 miles south of Baghdad. People, even Bible scholars, **confuse the Fall of Babylon with the Destruction of Babylon**. The Fall of Babylon happened in 539 B.C. The Persian king Cyrus, who captured the Medes in 549 B.C., took Babylon in 539 B.C. and Darius the Mede was his vassal-king. Babylon was taken over with military genius when the Euphrates River was re-routed so that the level of the moat system around the city was lowered, allowing the army of Cyrus to enter the city.

NOTICE: Josephus records that 12 days later Daniel presented Cyrus with a scroll (see Tanakh: Isaiah 44:28 and Isaiah 45:1-13) written **150 years earlier showing that God named Cyrus as the one who would release the Jews from the Babylonian exile to return to Jerusalem**. This ended the 70 year captivity prophesied ahead of time by Jeremiah the Prophet.

"And this whole land shall be a desolation, and an astonishment; and these nations shall serve the king of Babylon seventy years.

And it shall come to pass, when seventy years are accomplished, that I will punish the king of Babylon, and that nation, says Jehovah, for their iniquity, and the land of the Chaldeans; and I will make it **desolate** forever." **NOTE**: The Hebrew word "chorbah" here used for "**desolation**" means "**drought**." In other words, "**desert**." (Tanakh: Jeremiah 25:11-12)

Babylon was NOT destroyed. It became the second capital of Persia. Then, 200 years later it was Alexander the Great's capital. Through the years it has been withered but NOT destroyed with the kind of destruction the Bible foretells.

NOTICE: Isaiah Chapters 13 and 14—AND—Jeremiah Chapters 50 and 51 state that **Babylon will be destroyed like Sodom and Gomorrah. This has never happened. This is a FUTURE prophecy**. In **context** it shows that Israel is back in **their land**—the land of Israel—having been redeemed from the nations ... with, also, the goyim (strangers or gentiles). Babylon withered, but was never the recipient of destruction as prophesied. Even in the late 19th Century there were people living there. Saddam Hussein, over a period of 20 years, spent $60 million in rebuilding Babylon.

In 1983, Saddam Hussein started rebuilding the city on top of the old ruins (many artifacts and other finds were were built over and are under the city by now), investing in both restoration and new construction. He inscribed his name on many of the bricks in imitation of

Nebuchadnezzar. One frequent inscription reads: *"This was built by Saddam Hussein, son of Nebuchadnezzar, to glorify Iraq".*

This recalls the ziggurat at Ur, where each individual brick was stamped with "Ur-Nammu, king of Ur, who built the temple of Nanna". These bricks became sought after as collectors' items after the downfall of Hussein, and the ruins are no longer being restored to their original state. He also installed a huge portrait of himself and Nebuchadnezzar at the entrance to the ruins, and shored up Processional Way, a large boulevard of ancient stones, and the Lion of Babylon, a black rock sculpture about 2,600 years old.

When the Gulf War ended, Saddam wanted to build a modern palace, also over some old ruins; it was made in the pyramidal style of a Sumerian ziggurat. He named it Saddam Hill. In 2003, he was ready to begin the construction of a cable car line over Babylon when the invasion began and halted the project.

An article published in April 2006 states that UN officials and Iraqi leaders had plans for restoring Babylon, making it into a cultural center.

REMEMBER: Both Isaiah Chapters 13 and 14 AND Jeremiah Chapters 50 and 51 state that Babylon will be destroyed **like Sodom and Gomorrah**. This has never happened. This is a FUTURE prophecy.

THEREFORE: Babylon may be rebuilt, flourishing again.

HOWEVER: The Brit Chadashah (the New Testament) reveals the identity of New Babylon in Chapters 17 an 18.

IDENTITY OF NEW BABYLON

"And there came one of the seven angels which had the seven vials, and talked with me, saying unto me, Come here; I will show unto you the judgment of the great whore that sits upon many waters:

With whom the kings of the earth have committed fornication, and the inhabitants of the earth have been made drunk with the wine of her fornication.

So he carried me away in the spirit into the wilderness: and I saw a woman sit upon a scarlet colored beast, full of names of blasphemy, having seven heads and ten horns.

And the woman was arrayed in purple and scarlet color, and decked with gold and precious stones and pearls, having a golden cup in her hand full of abominations and filthiness of her fornication:

And upon her forehead was a name written, **MYSTERY, BABYLON THE GREAT, THE MOTHER OF HARLOTS AND ABOMINATIONS OF THE EARTH.**

And I saw the woman drunk with the blood of the holy people of G-d, and with the blood of the martyrs of

Yeshua (Jesus): and when I saw her, I wondered with great admiration."

— Brit Chadashah: Revelation 17, verses 1-6

There are seven keys to identifying Babylon, the Bitch. That is, there are KEY scriptural descriptions which inform us as to her geopolitical operations and location.

The Ruach Ha Kodesh—the Holy Spirit—revealed these to me years ago. I had never heard anyone teach about them and I had never read anything written by scholars about these keys. Almost every religious book, article, or commentary only described her as a religious system with origin and practices evolving from the ancient Babylon. However, **notice the following in Revelation Chapters 17 and 18** of the Brit Chadashah (the New Covenant, or New Testament):

א **Babylon is a literal city.** (Revelation 17:18 & 18:19)

ב **Babylon influences the leaders of the nations.** (Revelation 17:2, 18)

ג **Babylon, the Bitch, involves the nations and their inhabitants with fornication.** (Rev. 17:2) Note: the word "fornication" is the Greek "porneuo" which can mean sexual trade (also

20

human trafficking) or "illicit sexual intercourse or prostitution," and **is used both literally** (Mark 10:19, 1 Corinthians 6:18 & 10:8, Revelation 2:14 & 20) **and metaphorically** to describe spiritual fornication, or idolatry; for example, **false—anti God—religion, such as Islam.**

ד **Babylon is a seaport city.** (Revelation 18:17-19)

ה **Babylon is responsible for the murder of God's prophets and people who are slain upon earth.** (Revelation 17:6 & 18:24)

ו **Babylon is a key distributor of sorcery.** Sorcery can mean narcotics, witchcraft (magic arts) ... or idolatry, including spiritual deception. (Revelation 18:23)

ז **Babylon is THE KEY CENTER of world trade.** (Revelation 18:9-1)

On the next pages we will postulate a 12 Point Prophecy concerning New Babylon and her geopolitical ramifications.

IMPORTANT TO KNOW

The New World Governance—along with a major world religious system—will be bed fellows with the New Babylon ... AND **the New Nimrod: the False Messiah**.

The "cry" of the public around the world will be for peace and safety—the nations will gladly accept control—and **this will be the coup de grâce against Israel ... BUT ... G-d has other plans. Read on to see a 12 Point Prophecy.**

A 12 POINT PROPHECY

1. New Babylon will be rebuilt by the authority of a group of nation states (probably 10 regions) and then become headquarters for the New World Governance.

2. New Babylon will be the International Trade Centre of trade of trade (both legal and illegal).

3. New Babylon will be the international locus of drugs, pornography and the occult (including witchcraft).

4. New Babylon will be the centre of the New World Governance.

5. The 10 region governmental mandate that originally grants New Babylon her authority as a world center of world trade will also establish Babylon as the head of governmental religion.

6. The authorized "One World Religion" will have sub-powers under the administration of the **False Prophet**—who will be appointed by the leader of the New World Order—such as authority to execute Jews and (real) Christians ... AND ...

7. To execute by decapitation those who do NOT take the identification mark—**the name, number or number of the name**—of the world leader: the leader designated by the Confederacy of Nation States.

8. New Babylon will juxtapose herself with Jerusalem.

9. Babylon will eventually be **destroyed** by the **same** group of nation states—**probably 10 regions which evolve out of the New World Governance ... or the Ten Nation Islamic Confederacy, similar to *Al-Tahaluf Al-A'shari***—which originally gives the authority for New Babylon to be the epicenter of trade and religion.

10. This same group of the 10 nation states—*and others*—will attack Israel.

11. Messiah will destroy the group of nation states who attack Israel.

12. The Messianic Kingdom will be established and Messiah Yeshua will rule in peace from Jerusalem.

STUDY RESOURCE >>> For a detailed unabridged study of HOW Babylon—*a literal center of commerce AND religion*—will be Israel's greatest enemy in the End Times, study the book: ***Babylon the Bitch: Enemy of Israel***.

Also, to learn about the **secret mystery matrix** and its attempt to destroy Israel (past, present and future), study the book: ***Enhanced Humans: Mystery Matrix***.

Both books are shown later at the end of this book.

WHAT TO WATCH FOR

1. A world leader who is fatally wounded in the head AND whose deadly wound is healed. This leader will be the one the New World Governance will choose as their leader. **He will be the FALSE messiah**.

2. Or ... a world system which was seemingly dead is revived and becomes a great world power once again. **This could be Islam**. The Eastern leg of the Old Roman Empire outlived the Western leg for about 1,000 years. In the past, many Bible scholars tried to fit the Old Roman Empire into the 10 nation confederacy that will arise in the last days. However, they failed to take into consideration that **the Ottoman Empire—and Islam—was more destructive and covered more geographic area**. So, hermeneutically, Islam could be the exact "fit" for a **"deadly wound that was healed."** This **may be** the correct interpretation ... and therefore: **WATCH TURKEY AND ISLAM.**

3. Turkey may either be selected as a member of the EU – **OR** – will turn to the Islamic East for affiliation in worldwide commerce and trade.

4. The United Nations may move their headquarters to Turkey.

5. China will surpass Russia and the USA in nuclear proliferation and commerce and become part of the military triumvirate of the East.

6. A combination of the EU, the Arab League (previously League of Arab States) and Iran forming a complex of TEN Regions of nation-states.

7. New Babylon will become the concourse of world trade and Muslim ideology.

8. New Babylon **may be** located in Mecca, Saudi Arabia (41 miles from Jeddah Sea Port in the Red Sea. Jeddah may be dredged to facilitate increased international trade.) However, any of the following are good prospects:

> Istanbul, Turkey
> Dubai, UAE
> Rotterdam, Netherlands (near The Hague)
> New York, USA (present home of UN)
> London, UK

IMPORTANT

Attempts to place New Babylon at locations other than a seaport city are NOT accurate Biblical interpretation.

NOTICE

The majority of soldiers in the Roman Army who destroyed Jerusalem and the Temple in 70 AD / CE **were from Syria, Egypt and Arabia**. They were transcripts. These were *"the people of the prince who shall come"* described in Daniel 9:26. Therefore, **the "prince who shall come"**—*the false Messiah*—**may be from the Middle East**.

On the next pages we will look into Israel's recent history and how it aligns with its prophetic regathering.

28

ISRAEL AND END TIMES PROPHECY

If you want to know where we are in end time prophecy, **watch Israel**. Ever since the Regathering in the Land, we can see end-time prophecy unfolding. We see Jerusalem becoming the scriptural "Cup of Trembling." There have been **fifteen major conflicts** between Israel and its neighbors since the 1948 United Nations partition, as follows:

1. 1948 War of Independence—November 1947 - July 1949.

2. The retribution operations—conducted in the 1950s (Military response by Israel for every terror action made by the Fedayeen).

3. The Sinai War—October 1956.

4. Six-Day War—June 1967.

5. War of Attrition—1968-1970 (a limited war fought between the Israeli military and Egypt, the USSR and the PLO to recapture the Sinai from Israel).

6. Yom Kippur War—October 1973.

7. Operation Litani—March 1978 (The 1978 South Lebanon conflict).

8. First Lebanon War—Began June 1982.

9. The fighting in Southern Lebanon—1985 - 2000.

10. The First Intifada—Began in December 1987.

11. The Gulf War (1991)—Israel attacked by Iraqi missiles to provoke a response.

12. The al-Aqsa Intifada—Started in September 2000.

13. Second Lebanon War—Summer 2006.

14. Operation Cast Lead—2008-2009 (IDF strikes in the Gaza Strip in response to rocket attacks).

15. Israel and Hamas—November 2012 & 2014

Israel has to win every war to survive. The enemies of Israel do NOT have to win any wars to survive, except the last one. From a nuclear standpoint, Israel is a "one-bomb country." **One nuclear device detonated over Israel would devastate the country**.

This puts Israel in a very bad position. **There is no room for error in their foreign policy.** They feel if they make one mistake, it is the end of them as a nation, thus **giving new meaning to the slogan "Never Again."**

Now ... with Israel's stance as "Never again" ... let us ponder what to **expect** from the current and future world governments.

WHAT TO EXPECT FROM
THE WORLD GOVERNMENT

1. THE UN WILL TRY TO FORCE ISRAEL TO DISCLOSE / DISMANTLE NUCLEAR ARMS

In the not-too-far-distant future, **the United Nations will attempt to divert its "presumed" attention** on the nuclear goals, stratagem, potential, and ambitions of Iran ... **to Israel**. The UN will then begin **a tireless campaign to halt any production of nuclear weapons**. It will try **to force Israel to disclose and dismantle its nuclear storehouse of weaponry** and, also, join the **Nuclear Non-Proliferation Treaty (NPT)**. The previous head of the IAEA (International Atomic Energy Agency), **a Muslim**, said In October, 2009, *"Israel is the number one threat to the Middle East given the nuclear arms it possesses."*

Bret Stephens, a Wall Street Journal columnist, actually declared HOW such a situation could happen soon. While in office, the US President Obama had, as one of his goals, "global nuclear disarmament." The US President had NO military experience, and was seen in his "hopefulness" and gestures towards negotiations

32

with Iran, as evidencing a lack of astuteness—or reality—in geopolitics, especially as regards tyrants who are megalomaniacs like Achmadinejad and Khomeini. Bertrand Russell gives his interpretation of megalomania: *"The megalomaniac differs from the narcissist by the fact that he wishes to be powerful rather than charming, and seeks to be feared rather than loved. To this type belong many lunatics and most of the great men of history."*

NOTE: Concerning the Joint Comprehensive Plan of Action (JCPOA)—**alias the Iran Deal**—sent to congress, **there was no signature**. Obama hadn't signed it ... neither had any other nation representative.

What most people—even politicians—did not and do not know is that **there were NO signatures of the Iran deal**—yet, Obama gave billions to Iran which helps support terrorism and produce nukes to aim at Israel, USA and the West.

The forcing of Israel to disband its nuclear weaponry would be its death knell. **Russia would more than likely attempt to enforce such a UN directive, with Iran by its side**. The result would be a playing out of the prophecies of Ezekiel Chapters 38 and 39. Read on to find out *"What is Ezekiel saying for today?"*

2. THE UN WILL TRY TO CREATE A PALESTINIAN STATE BY FIAT

Two times the Palestinians have rejected "over-generous" peace offers by Israeli Prime Ministers Ehud Barak and Ehud Olmert. Instead of chastising the PA for NOT accepting these offers, the UN and other world leaders criticize Israel. During his office, US President Obama insisted that Israel:

- Return to its pre-1967 borders (which Israel won after being attacked);

- Divide Jerusalem; and,

- Allow Palestinians to have a state with contiguous borders which would divide Israel's legal and rightful boundary into two parts.

Underlying and paving the way for a Palestinian state created by fiat and NOT by law will be—*and has already started taking place*—the intervention of the UN and government leaders to stop Israel for developing new housing settlements in Israel's rightful land.

REMEMBER

Prophecy informs us that Jerusalem will be a "cup of trembling" to the nations.

> *"The burden of the word of the LORD for Israel, says the LORD, which stretches forth the heavens, and lays the foundation of the earth, and forms the spirit of man within him.*
>
> *Behold, I will make Jerusalem a cup of trembling unto all the people round about, when they shall be in the siege both against Judah and against Jerusalem.*
>
> *And in that day will I make Jerusalem a burdensome stone for all people: all that burden themselves with it shall be cut in pieces, though all the people of the earth be gathered together against it."* – Tanakh: Zechariah 12-1-3

WHAT IS EZEKIEL SAYING TODAY

1. Turkey, Iran, Russia and other Middle East and North East African nations will form an alliance to attack Israel. This we know for sure!

2. G-d will defeat this alliance of Magog and others on the hills of Israel, and leave only 17 percent of them.

3. It will take seven months to bury the dead bodies, and seven years to burn the implements of war (probably radioactive elements).

4. The victory for Israel will be so great and miraculous that ALL nations will realize that the G-d of Israel is the LORD.

NOTE: There will be an earthly Kingdom established *(after another great war where Messiah wipes out all the enemies of Israel)* where the Messiah rules from Jerusalem. All nations and their leaders must be subservient to the King. Study the book, ***Map of the End Times***. (See "Other Books by Prince Handley" at back.)

Ezekiel was a watchman for Israel, but more importantly for today.

G-D'S PLAN FOR ISRAEL

Let me remind you that G-d's plan for the Middle East is to:

1. Settle the Jews in Israel.

2. Give Jerusalem to Israel.

3. Destroy Babylon

4. Judge Mt. Seir and Edom.

5. Make it evident to all nations that G-d has brought Israel back from the diaspora to Israel.

> *"Therefore, behold, the days come, says the LORD, that it shall no more be said, The LORD lives, that brought up the children of Israel out of the land of Egypt;*
>
> *But, The LORD lives, that brought up the children of Israel from the land of the north, and from all the lands whither he had driven them: and I will bring them again into their land that I gave to their fathers."* (Jeremiah 16:14-15)

6. Bring a spiritual awakening among Israeli people.

7. Make Jerusalem a "cup of trembling" to all nations.

Land for peace is NOT G-d's plan for the Middle East. **Land for peace is a trap to weaken and position Israel into a limited area where she would have NO effective air response (defensive or offensive) operations**. This is **a planned stratagem for the annihilation for the State of Israel**, and any Israeli (or, other) leader who defends such a plan should be marked as a traitor to the State of Israel.

Not only that, but the land belongs to Israel by:

■ Promise from G-d (to Abraham); and,

■ Victory in war (1948, 1967 and 1973).

Now that we know Israel's history—including recent victories AND the present and future strategy of the New World Governance and enemy nations against Israel—in the next pages we can examine the **future news** for Israel.

38

THE FUTURE NEWS FOR ISRAEL ... NOW

When the coming world leader—appointed by the New Global Governance—takes over, he will make a treaty (a covenant) with Israel for seven years. Today, in addition to disease and famine issues, the leaders of the dominant nations are concerned with three (3) primary factors:

1. Attaining peace among nations and ethnic groups;

2. Guaranteeing the flow of oil; and,

3. Stopping terrorism and conflict in the Middle East (especially between Israel and the Palestinians).

However, the CHIEF bargaining factor will be the city of Jerusalem!

A Seven Year Treaty will be the coup de grace for Israel. What you should be watching for is Leadership: a leader who will seemingly have the solution for the Israeli - Palestinian conflict. This leader, appointed by the NWO will bring temporary peace and will convince the Jewish people to sign a seven (7) year treaty.

This is a stratagem designed for the annihilation of the People of Israel: the Jews.

In exchange for agreeing to this treaty negotiation, **Israel will be allowed to rebuild her Temple** on the Temple Mount. Then, after three and one half years (42 months) the NWO leader (the false Messiah) will do just what Antiochus Epiphanes did, who desecrated the Jewish Temple at the time of the Maccabean revolt. (Tanakh: Read Daniel 9:24-27 and Daniel 11:31 in the Tanakh.) The new world leader will go into the new rebuilt Temple and blaspheme G-d. Then, he will declare that he is G-d.

The 42 months which follow this event (the last half of the seven year covenant) will prove to be the worst time of persecution the Jews have ever known: **worse than they experienced during the Holocaust under Nazi Germany.**

The *Seven Year Treaty-Covenant* will be a trap to bring about the subjugation, persecution, and total annihilation of the Jewish People.

>>> NOTICE: During the last half of the seven years **many Jews will flee to Jordan** where they will be safe

40

from the anti-Messiah, the coming world leader. G-d causes a supernatural geological happening to take place to protect them from an attempt of the new world leader to extinguish the Jews **who have fled to Jordan**, to an area about three hours south of Amman. Then ... **Messiah returns to vanquish the enemies of Israel and set up His earthly Kingdom.**

SUMMARY

So now you know the history of Israel—her origin and evolution—**plus what's happening and will happen** to Israel and the Middle East in the future.

However, there is more. There is NOW and in the FUTURE a symbiosis of amalgamation of "behind-the-scenes" collusion of geopolitical and "other worldly" players with designs for Israel—**and for YOU and your family**—which will interweave to bring about the most serious control mechanisms never before known to mankind. They are: **Babylon** and **Enhanced Humans**.

For more information on ***Babylon the Bitch: Enemy of Israel*** and ***Enhanced Humans: Mystery Matrix***, consult the ***Companion Books*** at the end of this book.

OTHER BOOKS BY PRINCE HANDLEY

- Map of the End Times
- How to Do Great Works
- Flow Chart of Revelation
- Action Keys for Success
- Health and Healing Complete Guide to Wholeness
- Prophetic Calendar for Israel & Goyim: Thru 2023
- Healing Deliverance
- How to Receive God's Power with Gifts of the Spirit
- Healing for Mental and Physical Abuse
- Victory Over Opposition and Resistance
- Healing of Emotional Wounds
- How to Be Healed and Live in Divine Health
- Healing from Fear, Shame and Anger
- How to Receive Healing and Bring Healing to Others
- New Global Strategy: Enabling Missions
- The Art of Christian Warfare
- Success Cycles and Secrets
- New Testament Bible Studies (A Study Manual)
- Babylon the Bitch – Enemy of Israel
- Resurrection Multiplication – Miracle Production
- Faith and Quantum Physics – Your Future
- Conflict Healing – Relational Health
- Decision Making 101 – Know for Sure
- Total Person Toolbox
- Prophecy, Transition & Miracles
- Enhanced Humans – Mystery Matrix
- Israel and Middle East – Past Present Future
- Anarchy and Revolution: A Prophecy
- Real Miracles for Normal People
- Sexual Immorality: Addiction of Loss
- Healing Toolbox Plus: A to Z Workshop

AVAILABLE AT AMAZON AND OTHER BOOK STORES

UNIVERSITY OF EXCELLENCE PRESS
San Diego ■ London ■ Tel Aviv

BONUS

To help you, and to help you teach others, we have prepared FREE **Rabbinical Studies** at this site:

www.uofe.org/biblical-studies.html

The above are commentaries from **ancient** Jewish Rabbis that identify the Mashiach of Israel.

Also, to help you, and to help you teach others, you will find Bible Studies in English, Spanish and French.

■ English FREE Bible Studies

www.uofe.org/biblical-studies.html

■ Spanish FREE Bible Studies

www.uofe.org/biblical-studies.html

■ French FREE Bible Studies

www.uofe.org/biblical-studies.html

COMPANION BOOKS

We recommend you obtain these **companion books** for a complete understanding of End Time geopolitics:

Map of the End Times ... AND ... *Flow Chart of Revelation*, focus on the events AND the judgments that occur on Planet Earth during the end times. These are easy to follow **time-line** of the events described in *The Book of Revelation*.

Flow Chart of Revelation will **assist you in mentally memorizing** the events so you will be able to describe— *to walk thru*—the events of the Last Days and teach them to others.

Babylon the Bitch: Enemy of Israel describes in detail the coming geopolitical happenings that will affect Israel and Middle East, with focus on Babylon: her identity, support system and "other world" bed-fellows.

Prophetic Calendar for Israel and the Nations. This book is **a prophetic outlook for the immediate future through 2023**. You will need this information in the future!

Also, you will want to obtain, *Enhanced Humans: Mystery Matrix*, which describes—at this time—a hidden and well-planned geopolitical "behind–the-scenes" amalgamation—**a spiritual collusion both human and other-worldly**—that is being orchestrated to facilitate control ... of Israel ... and of YOU and your family.

Companion books to *Israel and Middle East*:

Map of the End Times

Flow Chart of Revelation

Prophetic Calendar for Israel and the Nations: Thru 2023

Babylon the Bitch: Enemy of Israel

Enhanced Humans: Mystery Matrix

Available at Amazon and other book stores

LIVE A LIFE OF EXCELLENCE

For seminars Email to:
mentorhelp@gmail.com

UNIVERSITY OF EXCELLENCE PRESS
San Diego ▪ London ▪ Tel Aviv

NOTE

We listen to our readers. Tell us what **new** subject matter you would like to see published. Email your ideas to: universityofexcellence@gmail.com

www.ingramcontent.com/pod-product-compliance
Lightning Source LLC
Chambersburg PA
CBHW060657280326
41933CB00012B/2223